CARAMEL BROWN

A COLLECTION OF POETRY AND PROSE

SHUBORNO CHAKROBORTY

To the unknown force that has helped me time and again to emerge from

extreme turmoil in the most creative manner.

Contents

Preface   *vii*

Acknowledgements   *ix*

  1. Love And Hatred   1

  2. Wings Of Infinity   3

  3. Won't Let You Go   5

  4. Lady Divine   9

  5. Caramel Brown   11

  6. The Maiden Of The Moon   13

  7. Sweet Heart   15

  8. We Never Met   18

  9. Love   20

10. Choice   22

11. Fall And Rise   24

12. Hope And Fear   26

13. Pain   28

14. Dilemma   30

15. Overcast Evenings   33

16. Angels And Demons   35

17. The Story Of A Droplet   37

18. Evenings Of March   39

19. Freedom In A Cage   42

20. On The Canvas Of My Existence   44

21. Being   46

22. Manifesting Greatness   48

23. Darkness   50

24. The Tainted Soul   52

Contents

25. Hope Never Ends		55
26. Under Trial		57
27. Independence		60
28. Sailor		62
29. The Timeless Wisdom		64
30. Strife		66
31. All I Have		68
32. Sleepless Nights		70
33. To Infinity And Beyond		72
34. Whispering Death		74
35. Once Upon A Time		76
36. Raging Fire		78
About the author		81

Preface

In 2019, I was at CBCS Allahabad, pursuing a master's in cognitive sciences. For one of our assignments in neuroscience, I chose creativity as the topic. While conducting a preliminary literature review on the brain and creativity, I came across an interesting concept: *"Pain-induced creativity."* I was thrilled because I had often noticed that during intense emotional events, my creative side would flare up. The intense need to express my innermost thoughts through writing has always been therapeutic for me.

I have published five books, including this one, and each has been the outcome of my mental and emotional struggles and turmoils. Poetry and prose have served as powerful ways to clear my mind. Many times, I have reached a point where self-harm seemed imminent, but writing has helped me move beyond that state. When you think deeply and try to understand the patterns of your life, your role in the universe, or when you're trying to let go and move on, writing can be incredibly healing.

We all face situations where misunderstandings become overwhelming, and the need to justify ourselves becomes urgent. When we cannot resolve those misunderstandings, the resulting mental and emotional pain can be extremely damaging. In these moments, the act of playing with words can be deeply satisfying and therapeutic.

In this collection, I focus on themes of love, life, passion, existence, anxieties, and depression. Of the thirty-six poems and prose pieces, the first fourteen address issues of relationships, love, sensuality, unrequited love, and emotional struggles. The remaining pieces explore anxieties, existential thoughts, and depression. I feel blessed that the universe has given me the ability to express myself through words—otherwise, this book might have been published by my ghost in some other realm.

Each chapter begins with an illustration and a quote. The illustrations (for the chapters as well as the back cover), developed using ChatGPT-4o, capture the essence of each chapter. The quotes, sourced from Goodreads and BrainyQuote, also serve to connect with the prose or poem in that chapter. This collection is the result of my experiences over the past two and a half years, during which I've navigated mostly the "downs" and a few "ups" in life.

Finally, the title of the collection, *Caramel Brown,* was inspired by one of the most emotional experiences I've been through in recent times. This experience sparked my creative drive to publish this collection. The term *"caramel brown"* refers to a color that combines the sweetness of caramel with the warmth, humility, and groundedness associated with brown. In my life, this color brought a brief phase of sweetness and flavor, only to leave me questioning my existence and purpose, pushing me to the point where I had to surrender to the universe.

I won't go into the details of my personal experiences, but this color holds great significance in shaping my understanding of my creative side, as well as my mental and emotional health. I truly hope you enjoy reading my expressions and experiences, captured in poetic form.

Acknowledgements

To my loving family, especially my elder brother, Mr Shubham Chakroborty, you have remained by my side, through my highs and lows, offering solace during the moments of doubt and celebrating every milestone with unbridled joy. Your unwavering faith in my abilities has fueled my determination to pursue my dreams and push the boundaries of my creativity.

To my experiences, you have been the reason behind the highs and lows in my life. Your majestic way of testing my limits through the fire of emotional turmoil and seemingly hopeless situations has helped me make a comeback each time with greater wisdom and learning than before. I eagerly await more such trials.

To my emotional vulnerabilities, to my impulsivities, to my overthinking mind, to my fickle-mindedness, to my unconventional career, to my loneliness, to my mood swings and most importantly, to my genes. This novella wouldn't have been possible without the perfect balance of all these. These are sources behind this creative madness.

1. Love and Hatred

Love does not claim possession, but gives freedom.- Rabindranath Tagore

"Cut me off, My sweetheart,

Into fine pieces of love and hatred,

Keep the ones you cherished,

Throw the ones you detest,

But keep some part of me, With you, Forever,

Take this knife and make a slice,

This time I won't fall, But I will rise,

Pains were supposed to be,

A part and parcel of life,

You gave me some, I gave some too,

You broke some trust, I broke some too,

But let the souls again intertwine,

The tests are on, severe and scorTo,

Let's pass it together,

But keep some part of me,

With you, Forever and ever."

2. Wings of Infinity

• 3 •

Love liberates. It doesn't just hold, that's ego. Love liberates- Maya Angelou

"As my little birdie spreads her wings to soar,

She rises high, a force to adore,

Unstoppable, untamed, with strength divine,

Her spirit fierce, her heart entwined.

With wings of steel, her independence grew,

Freedom's fire burns, tenacity shines through,

Fly higher, my little one, touch the moon's pale glow,

Explore the cosmos with your creative show.

But if someday, your wings succumb to fate,

And darkness claims you, with a painful weight,

Fear not, my birdie, for I'll be there to hold,

To catch your fall, to mend your wings of gold.

I'll nurse your wounds, revive your spirit's might,

Prepare you for the journey, through the darkest of night,

To fly again with a heart full of divinity,

But that time I will be beside you with my wings of infinity."

3. Won't let you go

•

So hold my hand tight. Hold my hand with confidence. For this love can last forever. For this love, we shall share it together. — Shelby Dawson

"*Hold my hand,*
I won't let you go,
I would cover your face,
Embrace you firmly to my heart,
Whenever fear runs through your head,
Hold my hand,
I won't let you go,
Don't panic,
Don't shiver,
I am closer to you than ever,
Feel the warmth of my breath,
On your shoulder,
On your neck,
My lips brushing your earrings,
You were mine,
You are mine,
You will remain mine,
Forever,
Don't worry,
Hold my hand,
I won't let you go,
When you feel down and out,
In a mess,
Clutched in and out,
Struggling with the dilemmas of life,
Do remember,
This old soul,
The grand cheerleader of yours,
Waiting with full force,

To wade away all those,

Problems and issues of your life,

Keep your calm,

Let me sink inside your soul,

Hold my hand firmly and tightly,

I won't let you go,

Keep me intact in your memories,

Make me a part of your,

Daily life schedule,

Let me also live,

Every moment of happiness,

Every moment of despair,

With you,

Make me yours,

A part of your soul,

Forever and ever, My love!

I will wait for you,

To unite with you,

To experience every sun rise,

To witness every sun set,

Together for this entire life and beyond,

Let's manifest to grow old together,

My dear love,

But for the time being,

Don't worry,

Hold my hand,

Feel my presence,

Feel this moment,

The moments of togetherness,

We shared,

Those moments of intimacy,

Those moments of love,

Those cuddles and hugs,

In one position for the entire night,

In each other's arm,

Sleeping in harmony,

Lost into each other's dreams,

Believe me my princess.

I don't want you to go,

I won't let you go. "

4. Lady Divine

•9•

We loved with a love that was more than love.— Edgar Allan Poe

"Kill me softly, oh lady divine,
With those dovey eyes of yours,

This heart skips a beat every time,
As I observe, the little rose matures,
And as the paints on my canvas, you embrace,
Spreading, all over your frame,
Fondling, relishing the lustrous fruits of grace,
Pulling the cascading hair, flaring up the flame!
As those lips get warmer!
Widening the lips of nature too!
Erupting across the universe like a warrior!
Oh you damsel, I have experienced the goddess within you!"

5. Caramel Brown

If I had a flower for every time I thought of you… I could walk through my garden forever. — Alfred, Lord Tennyson

"*The world got fumed with passion that night,*

When those wet tongues rolled,

Down through their necks and lips,

Holding the curvaceous canvas,

Of her melodious vast,

The golden rush ran through her body,

The wavy caramel brown, cascading,

Hair of hers,

Falling beside those gorgeous earrings,

Teasing those mighty curves,

As he thrust upon holding the soft voluptuous sculpture,

The rose bloomed widening apart,

Letting the stone of love to kiss the rose,

The fragrance of the union spread across the room,

The moment he galloped with vigorous streak,

Pulling back the silky strands,

The infectious voice reached up the sky,

Feeling the warmth within,

The lovers gazed at each other with a teasing smile."

6. The Maiden of the Moon

The moon was so beautiful that the ocean held up a mirror.— Ani
DiFranco

"*She walks,*
Like a symphony,
Adorned in black,
With stars in her attire,
In a cloak of night..

She smiles,
With a moonlit gleam,
With those dovey eyes,
Like a radiant dream.

She looks,
Like a graceful rhapsody,
Her cascading hair,
A waterfall's melody..

She glances,
Above the glasses,
Creating a hypnotic blue,
Smile on her lips,
Soft as petals,
With a rosy hue…

She is,
The maiden of the moon,
In a harmonious trance,
Nurturing the universe,
Flirting with the existence,
With her cosmic dance."

7. Sweet Heart

Your words are my food, your breath is my wine. You are everything
to me.— Sarah Bernhardt

Everything,
Yes sweetheart!

I am talking to you,
Absolutely everything,
Is out of your control,
Believe me!
So don't rush,
Listen carefully,
Think correctly,
Follow faithfully,
Expectations can kill your soul,
Be adaptable to the core,
Love yourself first,
Believe in the process,
On the journey...

Things may change,
In a jiffy,
There will be moments,
When you will find yourself,
Walking all alone,
In the dark and gloomy,
Road of life,
Untouched-Unheard,
Disgruntled-Disoriented,
But keep on walking,
The pains will change you,
Thickening your skin,
Preparing for your endeavors,
Yet to come…

Don't be a giver,

Be choosy, think before,

You proceed for your,

Act of kindness,

Not everybody deserve,

You may get stamped,

For vested interests,

To say the least,

So sweety!

Be cautious,

Be grateful,

Count your blessings,

Live in the moment,

Accept challenges,

Move on,

Be the best,

Version of yourself.

8. We never met

In all the world, there is no heart for me like yours. In all the world there is no love for you like mine.— Maya Angelou

"We never met,

We never felt closer to each other,
We never strolled through those city streets,
We never held hands while crossing those busy roads,
We never hugged, feeling those beats of love,
We never knew each others embarrassing secrets,
We never laughed our hearts out,
We never had those fights,
We never said sorry to each other,
We never knew our likes or dislikes,
We never kept talking till the wee hours,
We never felt uncomfortable in each other's presence,
We never knew each other well,
We never stopped talking to each other,
We never thought this would be the end.
"

9. Love

Love is like the wind, you can't see it but you can feel it.— Nicholas Sparks

Sacrificing its core to the sunshine,

Like the roots of the tree that intertwine,

Deep Down the earth they go,

Bearing the burden with silence,

Like the sun with a gentle glow,

Eroding the nightmares away mile by mile,

Devoid of any expectations,

That's how the love is like,

Pure and true,

A marvel to behold with wide eyes. "

10. Choice

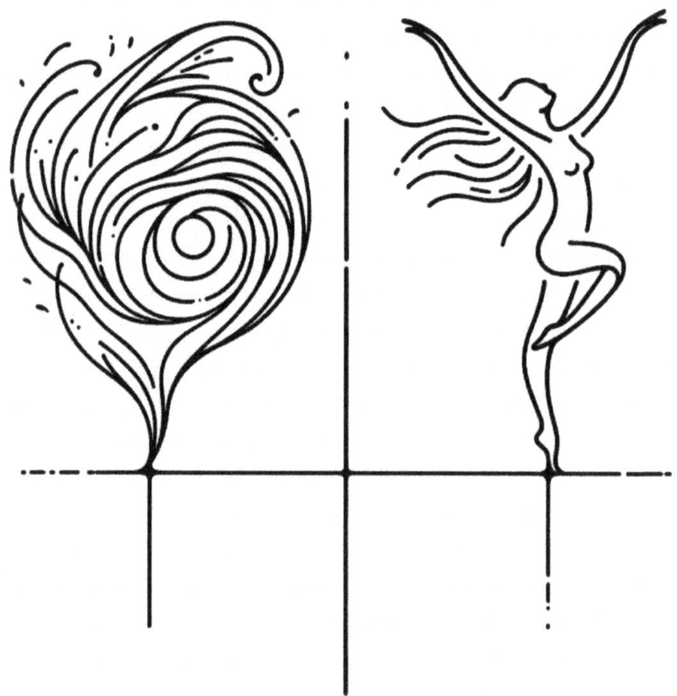

My love for you is past the mind, beyond my heart, and into my soul.— Boris Kodjoe

"I had two choices,

Either to fall,

Or to rise,

In love,

I chose the later,

After falling,

Way too deeper,

Into the forbidden, shallow,

Landscape of emotions,

Heads over heels. "

11. Fall and Rise

Love knows not distance; it hath no continent; its eyes are for the
stars.— Gilbert Parker

I fell,

I toppled,

I drowned,
Reached the bottom,
Of the mighty ocean of love,
There I found,
The gateway,
To the heavens,
And then,
I flew higher,
And higher,
Soaring above,
The clouds,
To touch the stars,
And,
I rose,
I rose,
I rose higher,
Than ever.

12. Hope and Fear

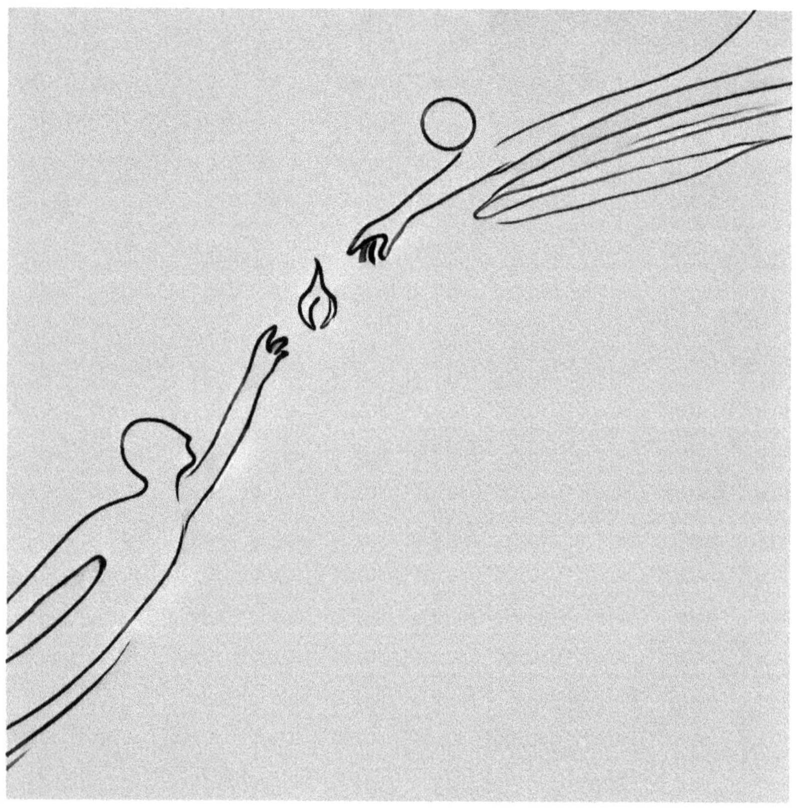

There is no remedy for love but to love more.— Henry David
Thoreau

"Hope, an uncertain path on a rocky terrain,

Fear, a slippery pass when it rains,
Desire, a fire inside the heart that burns,
Boiling with twists and melting with turns.
Peace, stranded alone, expressions aghast,
Love, enigmatic, silent, intricate and vast,
Grief, reverberates deeply with no bounds,
Tears, a tiny rivulet flows with no sounds,
Dreams, shattered reminders, under the skin,
Yearning and longing, a sour twinge within."

13. Pain

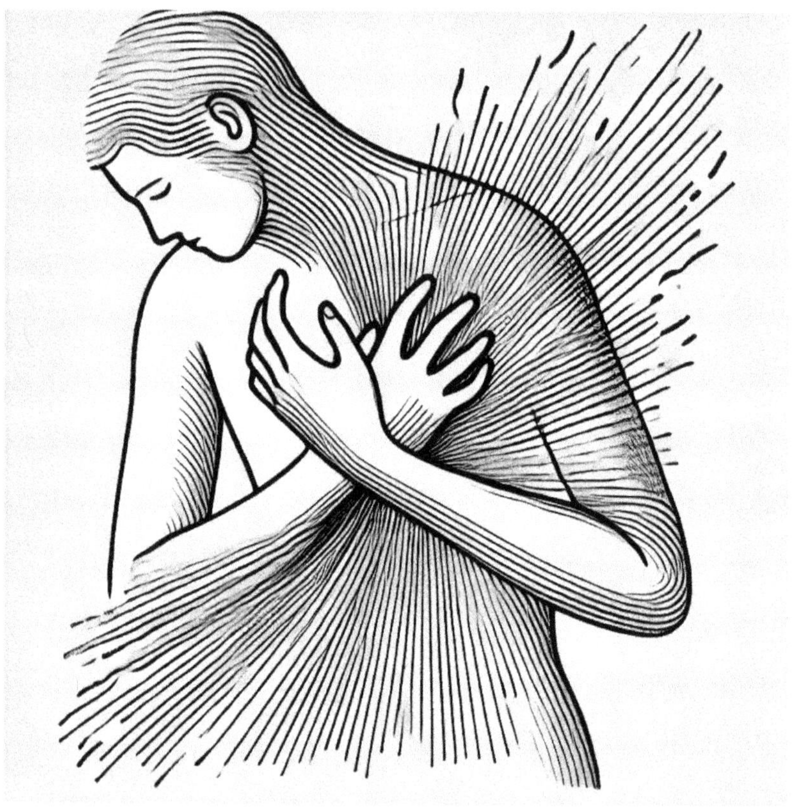

Turn your wounds into wisdom.— Oprah Winfrey

"*Pain,*

A cleanser,

A reminder,
Of liberation,
From,
The heartful cage,
The mental prison.
Where we hold on,
And dominate,
The bird,
Imprisoned,
So,
Set the bird free,
Let it fly,
Sky high,
With freedom,
Of love,
Breaking the shackles,
The illusion,
Of control,
To reach,
The treasure trove. "

14. Dilemma

At the innermost core of all loneliness is a deep and powerful yearning for union with one's lost self.— Brendan Behan

"*Walking with the crowd,*

In those busy streets,

Dancing with,

The musicians in retreats,

Searching for,

The one troubled within,

With my restless mind,

With my golden soul,

I saw the one,

With tears in those eyes,

Longing and yearning,

For a mighty surprise,

Exuberant and vivacious,

With full of joy within,

Maybe the restless mind,

Was finally at peace,

Putting forward my hands,

To lift her spirit,

Smiling with limitless,

Confidence and grit,

To tell the troubled one,

That here I was for her,

To turn off the phase,

Of loneliness and grieve,

The troubled soul,

Amused, charmed,

Took a deep breath first,

But backed off miles away,

With a sudden reprise,

An uninvited outburst,

Her voice got choked,

Tears fell straight away,

And She said,

That being without you,

Is so lonely

You can't even imagine,

But being with you,

Is even lonelier,

You would never understand. "

15. Overcast Evenings

In the middle of winter I at last discovered that there was in me an invincible summer.— Albert Camus

"*These overcast evenings…*

Relishes me to the core,

Surrounded by noise, a constant uproar.

Crows gossip around in darkening skies,

Panic-stricken cars with their honking cries.

The ashes of my cigarette fall with grace,

Smoke billows through, filling the space.

A cup of coffee sits, cold and forlorn,

As I idle away, feeling so worn.

Succumbing to loneliness, deep in its gloom,

In this quiet, empty, echoing room. ”

16. Angels and Demons

Pursue what catches your heart, not what catches your eyes.

— Roy T. Bennett

"I do have spring in my legs,
I hopped with enthusiasm in my veins,
Passing over the concrete jungle,
Reaching the destination to meet,

The brainiac beauty…
The angel and demon sitting over my shoulder,
Debated over something,
The demon said reach as soon as possible,
The angel said no, have patience wait for the response,
The mind was in a hurry to meet,
Even by crossing the ring of fire,
It ignored the angel's warning,
Who yawned and giggled,
Rolling on the floor,
Laughing out loud,
By looking at the man running,
Through the storm,
Passing by the crowd,
And it happened,
As it was supposed to be,
So be patient, wait for your turn,
Take these lessons for free. "

17. The Story of a droplet

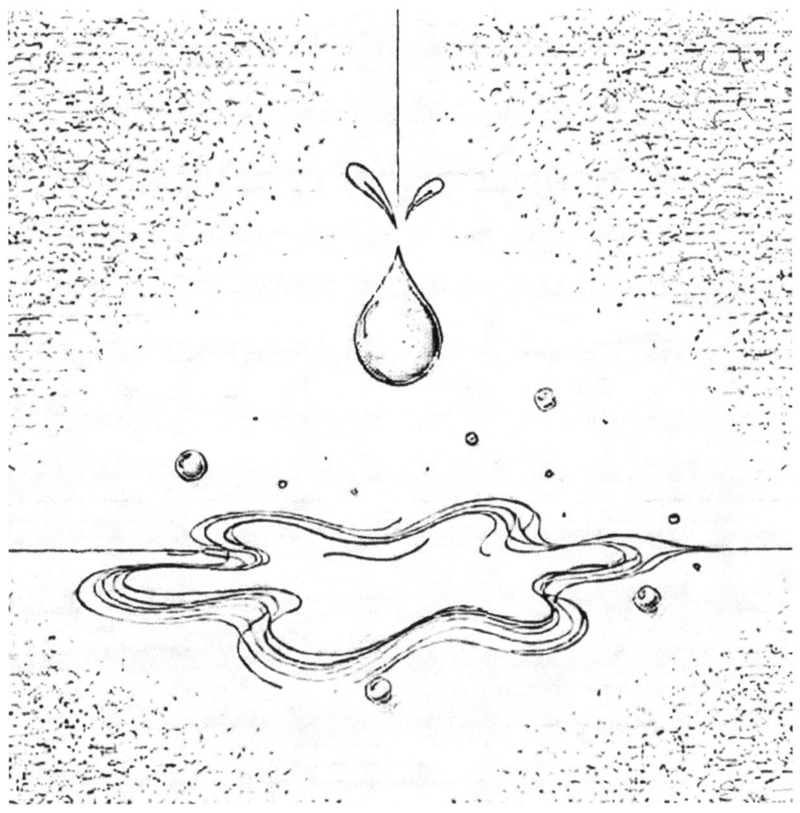

We must accept finite disappointment, but never lose infinite hope. – Martin Luther King, Jr.

"A drop of water,

Lost its way,

And fell,

On the surface of oil,

It stayed there long,

Interacting with

Innumerous oil-lets,

With due time,

It forgot its true nature,

It tried its level best,

To fit in,

Alas! Nature had already,

Played the spoilsport,

But it kept on trying,

To stick around,

As times passed,

The drop-let refused,

To accept,

Then one day it evaporated,

Into thin air,

To the place where it,

Actually belonged to,

Into the space,

Into the infinite.

"

18. Evenings of March

Memories and thoughts age, just as people do. But certain thoughts can never age, and certain memories can never fade. – Haruki Murakami

"Evenings

And memories

Of never ending march,

Once more

Fades away,

Leaving their mark..

As it gets,

Entrenched,

Deeper,

Into the mind,

In sweet and sour,

and soulful ways,

The trees,

Shed tears,

While the leaves,

Sways..

Scattered leaves,

And

Shattered lives,

Dried leaves,

Of expectations,

Each stepped upon..

As the poet,

Write the memoir,

Of an incorrigible clown..

He claims,

It takes time,

To blossom,

To grow,

To set,

The past aside,

To get back,

The gentle glow,

But,

He giggles,

And points out,

That,

What starts, must end,

What ends, shall peak,

Once again,

New flowers and leaves,

Must one shall seek..
"

19. Freedom in a cage

The only real prison is fear, and the only real freedom is freedom from fear. —Aung San Suu Kyi

"I raised a bird named freedom in a cage,

Atrocities abound, screaming in rage,
Breaking the shackles of thoughts and expressions,
It flew away and entered a bigger cage of ramifications,
Neither it could go left nor towards the right,
It got stuck in the center, noose tight. "

20. On the canvas of my existence

Life is not a problem to be solved, but a reality to be experienced.–
Soren Kierkegaard

"Out in the field,

When the darkness embraced my soul,

I saw thousands of twinkling stars,

Stuck in the heavens,

Lighting up the sky,

I closed my eyes,

But opened my vision,

To see within,

I found again,

Those brightening stars,

Illuminating my soul,

Projecting the entire universe,

On the canvas of my existence,

With seven shining sun's,

Balancing the earthy body,

Controlling the lunatic mind."

21. Being

The sole purpose of human existence is to kindle a light in the darkness of mere being. – Carl Jung

"*If you think, that you 'know',*
Then that means, you 'don't know',
If you think, that you 'don't know',
Then that means, you 'know',
The loop of 'knowing' and 'not knowing',
Is endless, It begins, where it ends,
A never ending saga of analysis-paralysis,
The unheard story of oxymoronic genesis,
So put a cut across the loop,
And jump across the states with realisation,
Without any need for dissemination,
The precise, objective, discrimination,
Of 'what is' and 'what is not',
So think carefully, decide correctly,
And follow faithfully,
That the 'being' has no contradiction."

22. Manifesting greatness

• 48 •

If your heart is broken, make art with the pieces.— Shane Koyczan

"*I survived the whimsical, weary winters,*

To reach a soulful, sweet spring,

But the almighty had some plans,

As I traversed through a scorching, silent summer,

Hither and thither in search of the soul,

Which burned deep inside, to resurrect,

To recreate, to help me taste the flavor,

Of the audacious, auspicious autumn,

Now, I'm waiting eagerly for the wild, wuthering winters,

With a delightful, enchanting mind,

To conquer the world both inside and outside,

Let's manifest greatness to conquer life. "

23. Darkness

In order for the light to shine so brightly, the darkness must be present. – Francis Bacon

"He quivered in the middle of the night,
He longed for the morning's light,
Spirits engulfed his nerves,
With their shrilling voice taking turns,
The mornings would be playful,
Chasing butterflies, so nice and cheerful,
Dancing to the tune of kindness,
Soothing voice, bubbling with brightness,
But betrayal and mockery was in his fate,
Crestfallen, despondent he would wait,
He retreated to the night's embrace,
Where darkness gave him shelter and space,
The spirits, ghouls, and banshees bowed,
To the king of anarchy they endowed,
The power to weave the mind,
He gradually became the darkest soul,
Satan's heir, his loving child."

24. The tainted soul

We are healed of a suffering only by experiencing it to the full. —
Marcel Proust

"Redesigning,

Resurrecting,

Recuperating,

The scar,

The wound,

The blemish,

The tainted soul,

But healing,

Takes time,

And time,

Heals,

The body,

The mind,

The physical,

The corporeal,

Existence, But…

What about the,

One, Out of,

The clutches,

The boundaries,

The territories,

Of matter and mind?

Traveling since ages,

When universe,

Was a speckle,

When time,

Had no time,

To keep a track,

Of debts and loans,

Taken by the soul,

To carry the voyage,
Of cause and effect…
The baggage,
We all carry,
On these weary shoulders,
Demands a final showdown,
To offload,
By repaying,
By bringing,
The curtains down,
By breaking,
The boundaries,
Of ethics and morals,
Halting the process,
Of sins and good deeds,
Finally,
It's time again,
To move on,
To experience,
Those hounds,
Barking around."

25. Hope never ends

For all sad words of tongue and pen, The saddest are these, 'It might have been'.— John Greenleaf Whittier

"If the hope,

Never ends,

Strangulate it,

With a rope,

Full of thorns,

Put the noose,

On flames,

It must bring it,

Down to ashes,

To never let it come back,

Let it scream as much,

As it could,

Kill the hopes,

Annihilate the desires,

If still,

The emasculated hope,

Try to survive,

Cut down its life force,

It will never,

Dare to revive. "

26. Under Trial

You have to understand that people have to pay a price for peace. If you dare to struggle, you dare to win. — Fred Hampton

"*Never imagined,*

Being selfless is a crime,

In the worlds of mere mortals,

Howsoever you try to prove,

You just can't,

Explanations remain unjust,

One can't dissect the body to show,

The truth,

Which hides inside the heart,

Even if we cut it apart,

It will just be a pound of flesh,

With blood splattered all around,

The truth which you know,

Would be unseen,

Hidden somewhere in the corner,

Of the heart,

But where does this heart exist?,

Who has the vision to see through?,

Into the layers,

It's only me,

Only me,

Me, the heathen poet,

Unjustified,

Unexplained,

Unexplored,

Under the trial of life,

Walking through the fire,

Burning, screaming deep inside,

Waiting for justice to be served,

By the heavens,

Only the gods know,

What's deep inside this mortal outfit,

The Kangaroo court,

Of the pretentious society,

With their flimsy virtues,

Fallacious ethical mockery,

Would never understand,

This pure soul,

It's time to bid adieu,

To the world of impermanence. "

27. Independence

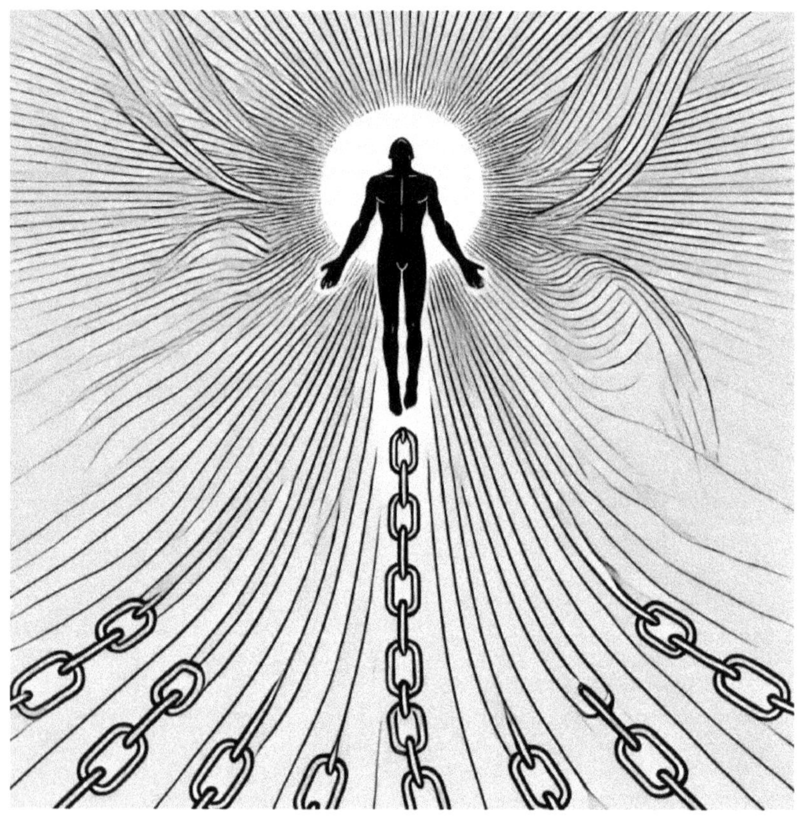

Originality is independence, not rebellion; it is sincerity, not antagonism.— George Henry Lewes

"*May we get independence from,*

The shackles of our mind and embrace the freedom in the soul,
May we rise higher and higher above all norms, caste, creed and
societal insecurity,
May we redefine our existence to hold our faith to the one who sees
through everything,
May we attain the higher wisdom, free from the boundaries of our
intellectual prowess,
May we resurrect ourselves and move ahead from the past,
Focusing on our present while designing a better future,
May we accept life the way it is. "

28. Sailor

We are imprisoned in the realm of life, like a sailor on his tiny boat, on an infinite ocean.— Anna Freud

"Listen,
To the harmony,
Of the burbling water,
The sailor makes merry,
By observing,
The non turbulent flow,
The sun shines,
Over the head,
With cool humid breeze,
Uplifting the minds,
Also the spirits,
The sailor enjoys,
The pristine weather,
But few knows,
How does it feel like,
Riding alone on a boat,
In the middle of the ocean,
In the shadowy night,
When waves,
Hit the shore,
With all its might."

29. The Timeless Wisdom

• 64 •

The only true wisdom is in knowing you know nothing.— Socrates

"*To be or not to be,*
The two faced option,

The heavens granted us,
We must remind ourselves,
That pain is inevitable,
But suffering is a choice,
The timeless wisdom,
The wise man ushered,
That life is impermanent,
Clouded with uncertainty,
Perishable to its core,
Estrangement is irreconcilable,
Independent of any stronghold,
Momentariness must be,
The heathen truth,
Irrevocably bound to the soul,
The illusory illumination,
Of the bewildered attachments,
May emboss an unmendable sole. "

30. Strife

We must never forget that there is always a new melody, a new tune, a fresh star.— Rita Marley

"Let us put,

An end,

To this,

Unending night,

Unstable plight,

Looking into my eyes,

Let us put,

An end,

To this,

Unbearable strife,

Unceremonious life,

These laments and cries,

Let us put,

An end,

To this,

Unscrupulous expedition,

Unnecessary trepidation,

Cutting all ties,

Let us put,

An end,

To this,

Unrealistic expectation,

Untimely subjugation,

From the ones,

Reeling in disguise."

31. All I have

I don't fear death so much as I fear its prologues: loneliness, decrepitude, pain, debilitation, depression, senility. After a few years of those, I imagine death presents like a holiday at the beach.— Mary Roach

"All I have,

Is a plummeting mind,

A heavy heart,

And a numb soul,

In this,

Dilapidated frame,

All I need,

Is a peaceful existence,

With a twinkling eye,

And a beaming smile,

On this,

Charming countenance,

But,

All I get,

Is a sorrowful trip,

Into the wilderness,

An emotional voyage,

In this,

Teary realm."

32. Sleepless Nights

The woods are lovely, dark and deep. But I have promises to keep, and miles to go before I sleep.— Robert Frost

"And the night begins once more,

As the slumber's hold starts to fade,

Bringing the demons, they soar,

Dancing to the hellish tunes of shade,

Tightening noose with dreams they stole,

Preparing the fire for the prey,

To burn this tormented soul,

The dawn looks so far far away,

This darkness, This unending shroud,

Plays with the storm without refrain,

Tomorrow the sun may get lost in the cloud,

It seems the bird won't chirp again,

As this heart awaits a bright morning,

Waiting for the flowers to initiate the dawn,

To put an end to this painful mourning,

Tiring it is, Wish this soul was never born. "

33. To Infinity and Beyond

Hope is a waking dream.— Aristotle

"Life has,

An expiry date,

With no labels on it,

Eventually everything,

Will come to an end,

All of a sudden,

That is,

The ultimate truth,

When immortality,

Will perish,

Waking us,

From the,

Dream,

For,

A voyage,

All over again,

With new set of,

Stories to share,

To write,

To create,

So don't get stuck,

In this beautiful dream,

Cherish the life,

The way it is,

Ends are followed,

By new beginnings,

The cycle of eternity,

Will keep moving on,

To the infinity,

And beyond.

"

34. Whispering Death

Some people die at 25 and aren't buried until 75.— Benjamin Franklin

"Amidst,

The echoes,

Of Silence,

I yearn for,

The whispering death,

Slowly it arrives,

At the door I sense,

Bringing gifts,

I anticipate,

A magical potion,

A cerebral poison,

Injecting slowly,

Into my breath,

When this mortal decor,

Turns blue,

It rejoices,

With exuberance,

As I try to escape the noose,

It mocks with a derisive grin,

On my fate,

Over time I accept,

This disdainful life,

As I go deeper,

Into the Abyss of aloneness,

While humming the lone wanderer's,

Mournful melody,

I accept,

The end of this existence."

35. Once upon a time

Far away there in the sunshine are my highest aspirations. I may not reach them, but I can look up and see their beauty, believe in them, and try to follow where they lead.— Louisa May Alcott

"Once

Upon

A time,

I aspired

To be

The one,

To reach

The stars,

To abolish

The darkness,

Dazzling

With brilliance.

The midnight summer,

Shooing

The murkier shadows

Screaming within,

With thousand splendid suns,

Never imagined

The racking dusk

Would engulf

This core,

Where

I lived

Once."

36. Raging Fire

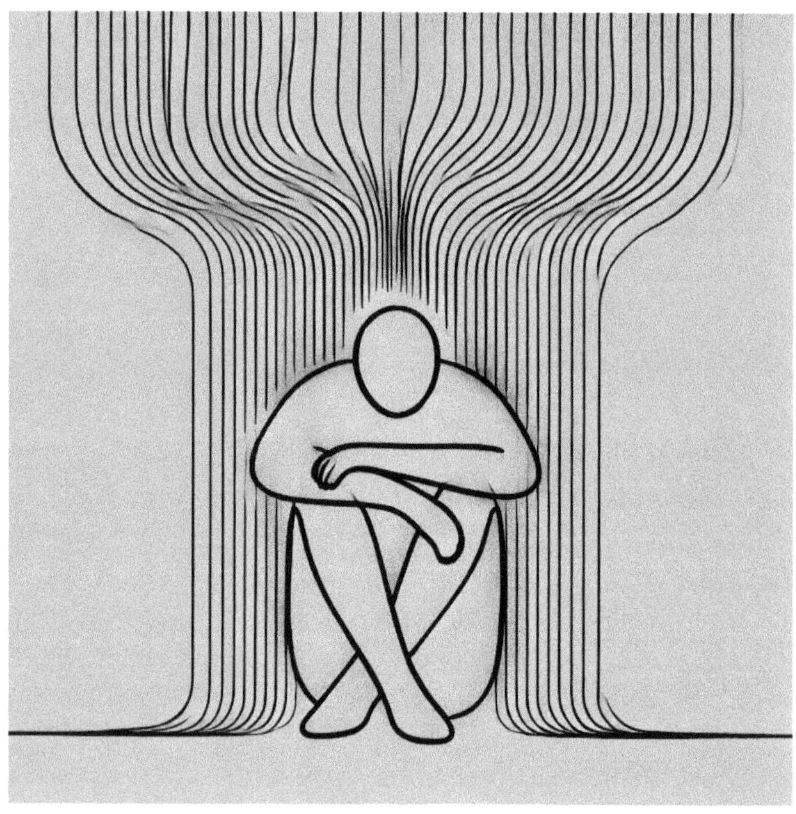

Do not brood over your past mistakes and failures as this will only fill your mind with grief, regret and depression. Do not repeat them in the future.— Swami Sivananda

"*As I sit over the flames,*

This disgusting attire burns,

And I endlessly wait,

For the untimely rains,

Me and my observant eyes,

Keeps a watch,

As this holy life turns,

Chaotic and Indecent.

Suddenly the pangs of destitution hits,

While alluring the world,

Yet the hungry, fidgety soul,

Asks for more,

Sways away into wilderness,

Like a sinner with unholy desire,

Attains the momentary lapse of sense,

Finds no way,

To stop this raging fire.

As the aroma of my charred flesh,

Gets recklessly intense,

Diffusing the room,

With its nauseating grace,

Now no more the soul laments,

But loves the excruciating,

Yet orgasmic ecstasy,

And blasphemous elegance,

Embraces the slumber,

Goes up in smoke and leaves behind,

The unchaste legacy.
"

About The Author

Shuborno Chakroborty is a versatile writer and thinker with a deep passion for exploring the intersection of science, technology, philosophy, and the human experience. He has published four books: *The Lost Prophet*, a collection of poems available on Amazon KDP; *The Divine Comedy*, a compilation of short stories and microfictions, *Space and Silence*, a collection of flash fiction and essays published by Notion Press; and *Mythical Sunshine*, a novella published by Notion Press. Shuborno's writing reflects his multidisciplinary thought process, blending his varied interests into compelling poems and fiction that challenge readers to think beyond the ordinary.

Shuborno has an interdisciplinary academic background, holding a BSc (Honors) in Physics from the University of Delhi, a master's in Cognitive Science from the Centre of Behavioural and Cognitive Sciences, Allahabad, and a master's in Public Policy (Science, Technology, and Innovation) from the Indian Institute of Technology, New Delhi.

Currently, Shuborno is a guest faculty member at the School of Public Policy, IIT Delhi, where he teaches a refresher course on applied mathematics. In addition to his academic role, he serves as director of Inscope Social Foundation, a Section 8 company dedicated to cultivating an innovative mindset and promoting science communication at the grassroots level. He is also a freelance author and mathematics popularizer for Pearson Education, India, and has co-authored the middle school mathematics textbook Maths-Ace Prime. Shuborno has organized several workshops for teachers and students across the country. Recently, he completed a stint at the Asian University for Women in Chittagong, Bangladesh, where he taught and trained pre-college students in applications of mathematics and creative problem-solving.

Shuborno was also invited to the Naval War College in Goa for Naval Higher Command Courses (NHCC-34, 36) by the Indian Navy to lecture on leadership, creative thinking, and basic statistics to navy and army officers. He has delivered lectures for the National Institute of Open Schooling (NIOS) on topics in applied psychology.

Shuborno's unique voice and perspective continue to captivate audiences as he weaves together the mysteries of the universe, the intricacies of the human mind and behavior, and the ever-evolving landscape of society and technology.

www.ingramcontent.com/pod-product-compliance
Lightning Source LLC
Chambersburg PA
CBHW040825120726
48005CB00012B/1505